Influential Presidents

Abraham Lincoln

by Martha London

www.focusreaders.com

Copyright © 2023 by Focus Readers®, Lake Elmo, MN 55042. All rights reserved. No part of this book may be reproduced or utilized in any form or by any means without written permission from the publisher.

Focus Readers is distributed by North Star Editions:
sales@northstareditions.com | 888-417-0195

Produced for Focus Readers by Red Line Editorial.

Photographs ©: Shutterstock Images, cover, 1, 4, 7, 19, 20–21, 22, 25, 27, 29; Eastman Johnson/W. Harring. & L. Prang & Co./Library of Congress, 8; North Wind Picture Archives/Alamy, 11; Old Paper Studios/Alamy, 13; Strobridge & Co./Library of Congress, 14; Fotosearch/Getty Images, 17

Library of Congress Cataloging-in-Publication Data
Names: London, Martha, author.
Title: Abraham Lincoln / Martha London.
Description: Lake Elmo, MN : Focus Readers, [2023] | Series: Influential presidents | Includes bibliographical references and index. | Audience: Grades 2-3
Identifiers: LCCN 2022026065 (print) | LCCN 2022026066 (ebook) | ISBN 9781637394656 (hardcover) | ISBN 9781637395028 (paperback) | ISBN 9781637395738 (ebook pdf) | ISBN 9781637395394 (hosted ebook)
Subjects: LCSH: Lincoln, Abraham, 1809-1865--Juvenile literature. | Presidents--United States--Biography--Juvenile literature. | United States--History--Civil War, 1861-1865--Juvenile literature. | United States--Politics and government--1861-1865--Juvenile literature.
Classification: LCC E457.905 .L65 2023 (print) | LCC E457.905 (ebook) | DDC 973.7092 [B]--dc23/eng/20220606
LC record available at https://lccn.loc.gov/2022026065
LC ebook record available at https://lccn.loc.gov/2022026066

Printed in the United States of America
Mankato, MN
012023

About the Author

Martha London is a writer and educator. She lives in Minnesota with her cat.

Table of Contents

CHAPTER 1
Speaking at Gettysburg 5

CHAPTER 2
Self-Taught Lawmaker 9

CHAPTER 3
The Civil War 15

ISSUE SPOTLIGHT
Emancipation 20

CHAPTER 4
One Union 23

Focus on Abraham Lincoln • 28
Glossary • 30
To Learn More • 31
Index • 32

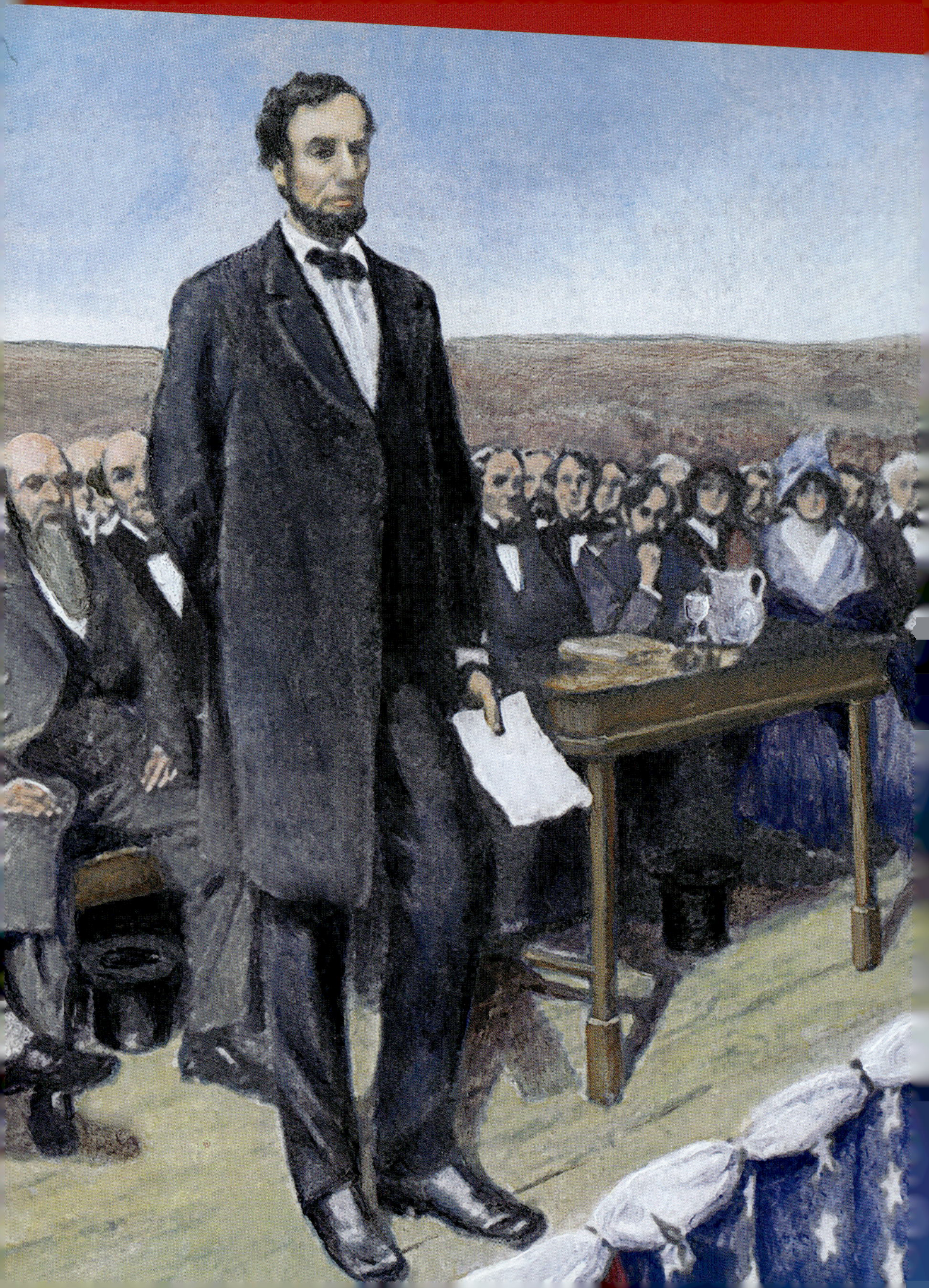

Chapter 1

Speaking at Gettysburg

In November 1863, President Abraham Lincoln prepared to give a speech. He was in Gettysburg, Pennsylvania. Four months earlier, a major battle had taken place there.

▶ **Lincoln's speech became known as the Gettysburg Address.**

The battle was part of the US Civil War (1861–1865). Southern states wanted to form a new country. They planned to keep slavery legal. Northern states did not want the United States to split apart. So, the two sides went to war.

Many people died in Gettysburg. The battlefield became a **cemetery**.

Did You Know?

More than 50,000 people were hurt or killed in the Battle of Gettysburg.

> Today, a large monument stands near the spot where Lincoln gave his speech.

Lincoln spoke there. He said the United States would remain one country. He said all people should be free.

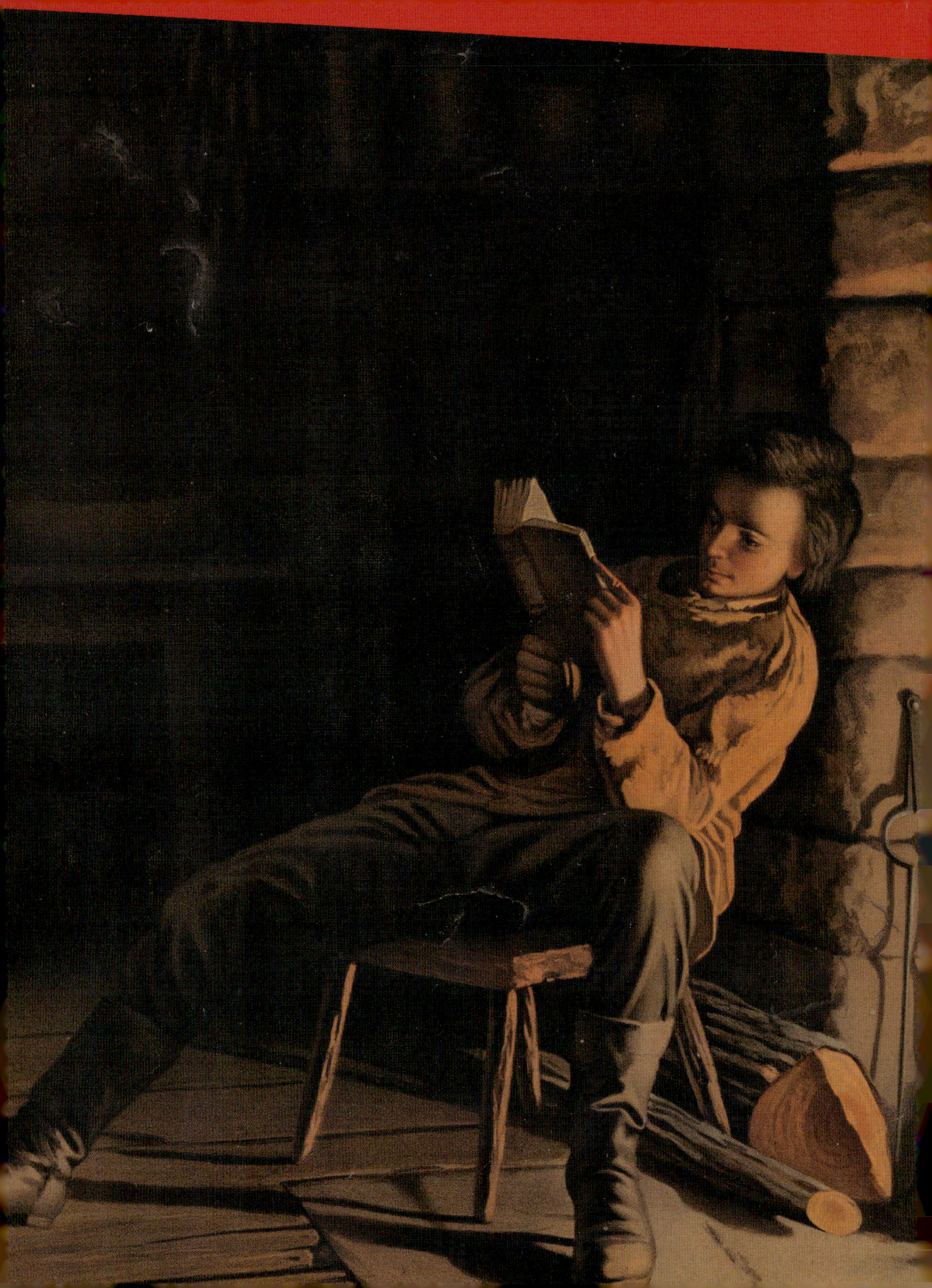

Chapter 2

Self-Taught Lawmaker

Abraham Lincoln was born on February 12, 1809. He grew up in Kentucky and Indiana. Abraham did not go to school. Instead, he worked on his family's farm. He taught himself to read and write.

▶ **As a boy, Abraham Lincoln enjoyed reading.**

Lincoln moved to Illinois when he was 21. He tried many different jobs. In 1834, Lincoln won an election. He became a lawmaker. He worked for the state of Illinois. Lincoln held this job for eight years. He pushed for better railroads and **canals**.

Did You Know?

Lincoln became a lawyer in 1836. But he didn't go to law school. Instead, he studied and passed the test on his own.

▶ **As a young man, Lincoln worked on a boat that carried goods down a river.**

In 1846, Lincoln was elected to the US Congress. At this time, the United States was at war with Mexico. Lincoln spoke out against it.

11

Lincoln served in Congress for two years. He went back to Illinois when his **term** ended. However, he wanted to work in government again.

In 1858, Lincoln ran for the US Senate. He lost to Stephen Douglas. Even so, leaders in the Republican **Party** were impressed. They saw

Did You Know?
Large crowds gathered to watch Lincoln and Douglas speak in 1858.

> A crowd watches Lincoln and Douglas talk about their ideas.

that Lincoln was a skilled speaker. He was easy to understand. And he connected with voters. In 1860, the Republicans picked Lincoln to run for president.

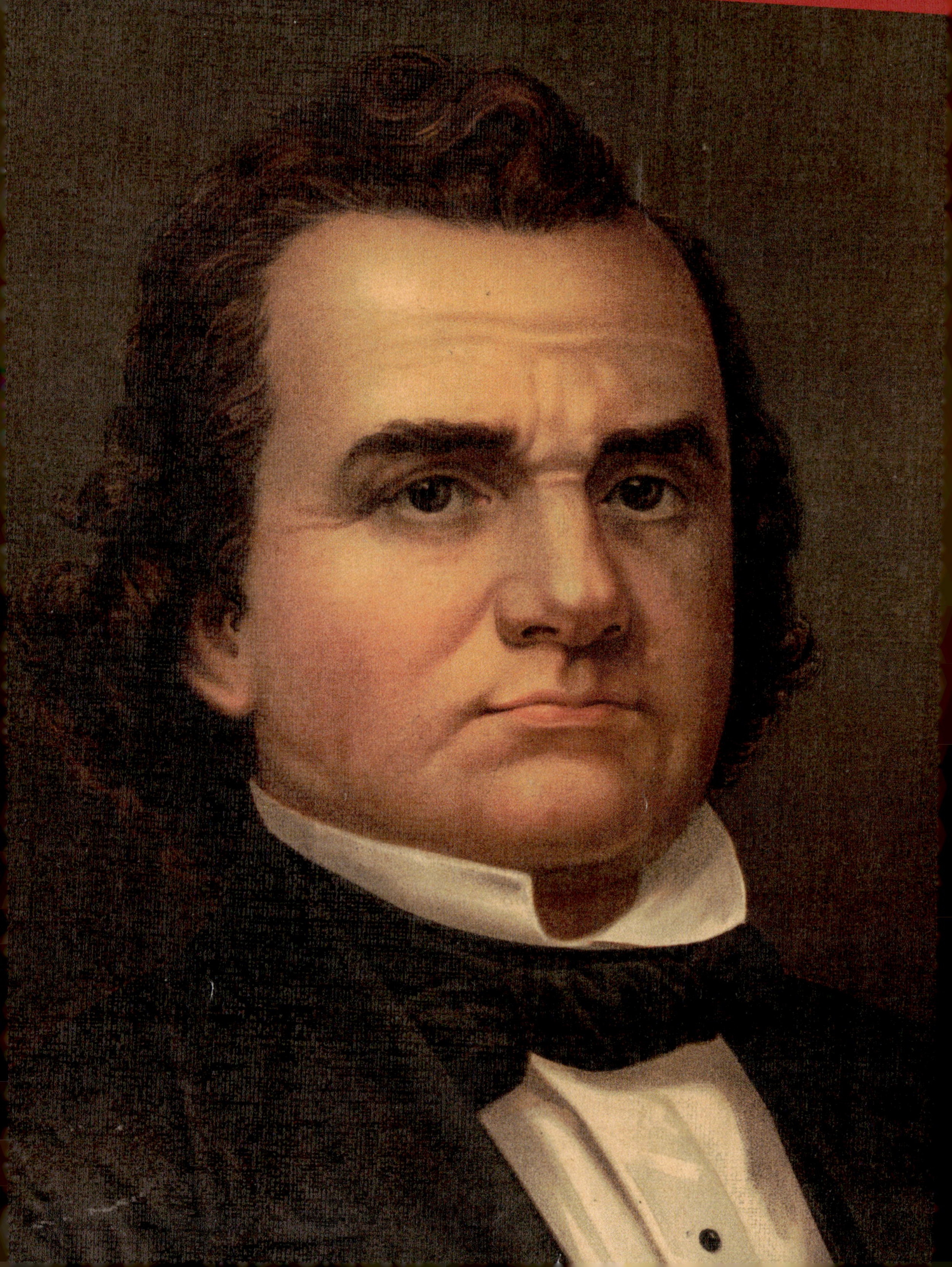

Chapter 3

The Civil War

In 1860, voters were divided. They could not agree about slavery. Some states allowed it. Other states did not. Four people were running for president. Three of them did not want to end slavery.

▶ **Stephen Douglas was one of the four people who ran for president in 1860.**

Abraham Lincoln disagreed. He believed slavery was wrong. But he didn't think the national government could end slavery. Instead, he thought states had that power. So, Lincoln wanted to make slavery illegal in new states. In this way, he hoped slavery would end slowly over time.

Did You Know?

In 1861, there were more than four million enslaved Black people in the United States.

> **White slaveholders forced Black people to do backbreaking work.**

Lincoln won the election. But he was very unpopular with white people in the South. They feared he would make slavery illegal everywhere in the country.

For this reason, most Southern states left the Union. They wanted to form a new country. It would let white people hold slaves.

In April 1861, the Civil War began. At first, Lincoln had one main goal. He hoped to keep the Southern states in the Union. But

Did You Know?

In 1862, Lincoln said Black people should leave the United States when they were freed.

▶ **In 1863, the Union army started allowing Black soldiers to join.**

the war continued for many months. Over time, Lincoln's views on slavery changed. He added another goal. He said slavery should end in all states. And this change should happen right away.

19

ISSUE SPOTLIGHT

Emancipation

Lincoln gave an order in 1863. He said slavery was illegal in the states that had left the Union. But Lincoln could not force those states to follow his order. So, most enslaved people were not freed right away.

On June 19, 1865, Union soldiers arrived in Texas. That was the last Southern state to come under Union control. Black people were now free across the South. June 19 became known as Juneteenth. Today, people still celebrate this day.

Lincoln's order was called the Emancipation Proclamation.

21

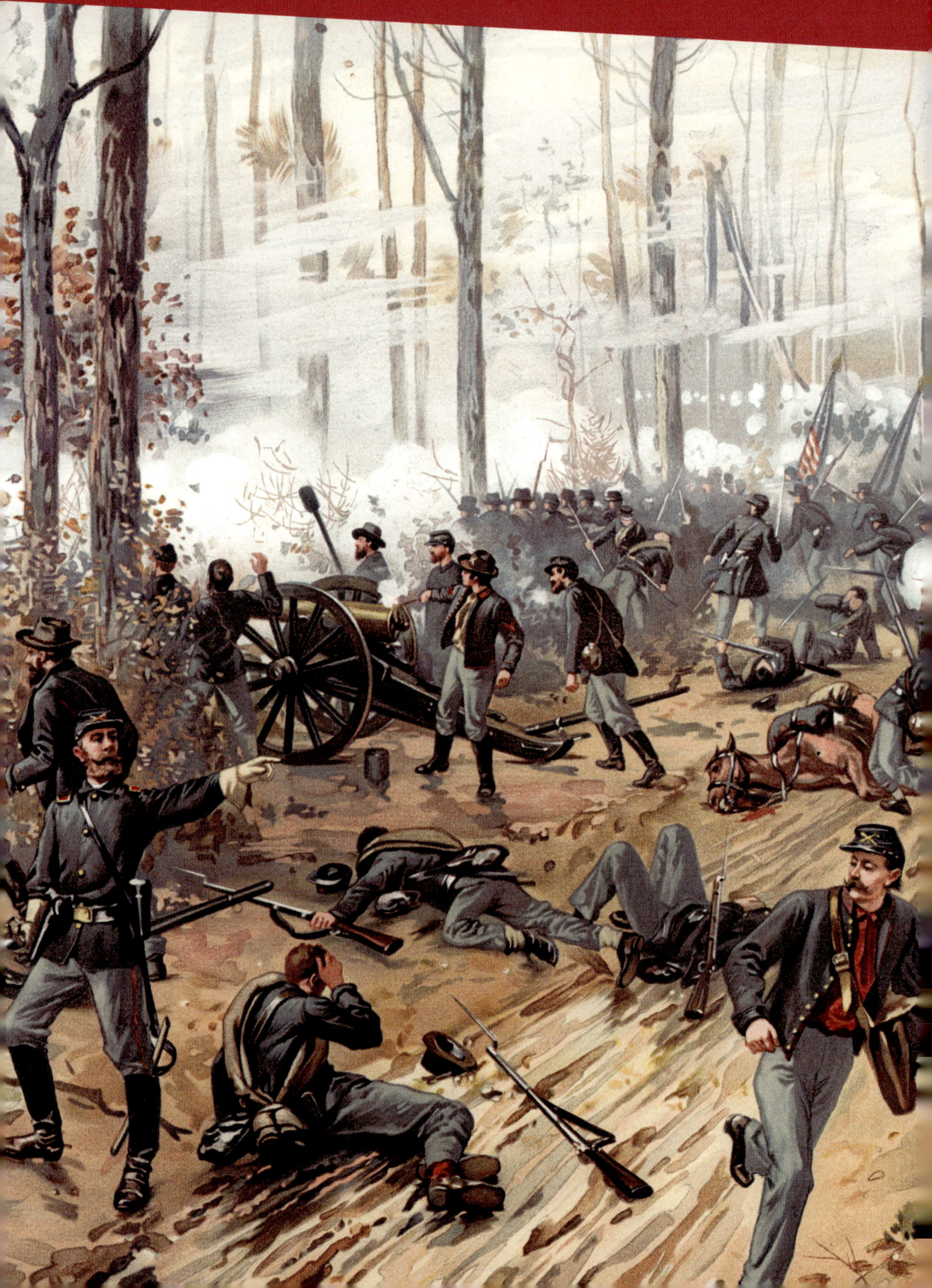

Chapter 4

One Union

The Civil War continued into 1864. That year, Abraham Lincoln ran for president again. He won easily. He received many votes in the North. Most Southern states were still fighting. So, they didn't vote.

> **More than 600,000 people died during the Civil War.**

In April 1865, the Southern states gave up. The Civil War was finally over. Lincoln had just started his second term. He knew there was a lot of work to do. Many cities had been ruined during the war. Many farms had been burned.

Rebuilding was going to be difficult. Healing the country would be even harder. But Lincoln never got the chance to try. He was shot by a man who supported slavery. Lincoln died on April 15, 1865.

▶ **Lincoln's killer shot him while he was watching a play.**

Today, people remember Lincoln for keeping the United States together. They also remember his work to end slavery.

25

Before Lincoln died, he had pushed for a new **amendment**. He wanted slavery to be illegal everywhere in the United States. In late 1865, the Thirteenth Amendment made that happen.

Other changes followed. In 1868, the Fourteenth Amendment made

Did You Know?

The Thirteenth Amendment ended slavery. But people can still be forced to work as punishment for a crime.

> In 1870, Hiram Revels became the first Black lawmaker in the US Congress.

Black people US **citizens**. And in 1870, the Fifteenth Amendment gave Black men the right to vote. Today, Black Americans continue to fight for **equality**.

FOCUS ON
Abraham Lincoln

Write your answers on a separate piece of paper.

1. Write a sentence that describes the main ideas of Chapter 3.
2. Why do you think Lincoln's views on slavery changed over time?
3. When was Lincoln elected to the US Congress?
   - **A.** 1834
   - **B.** 1846
   - **C.** 1858
4. Why did Southern states try to form a new country after Lincoln was elected?
   - **A.** They wanted slavery to end slowly over time.
   - **B.** They wanted to keep slavery legal.
   - **C.** They wanted to start a war with the North.

5. What does **served** mean in this book?

*Lincoln **served** in Congress for two years. He went back to Illinois when his term ended.*

    A. started a civil war
    B. worked in government
    C. traveled to a new place

6. What does **divided** mean in this book?

*In 1860, voters were **divided**. They could not agree about slavery.*

    A. all thinking the same thing
    B. forced to work without pay
    C. unable to agree on an idea

Answer key on page 32.

Glossary

amendment

A change or addition to a legal document.

canals

Long, human-made ditches that allow water to flow from one area to another.

cemetery

A place where dead people are buried.

citizens

People who are official members of a certain country and have specific rights as a result.

equality

Fair treatment, with the same rights as others.

party

A group that has specific ideas about how the government should be run.

term

The amount of time a person can serve after being elected.

To Learn More

BOOKS

Lynch, Seth. *The Emancipation Proclamation*. New York: Gareth Stevens Publishing, 2018.

Murray, Laura K. *Abraham Lincoln*. Mankato, MN: Capstone Press, 2020.

Rumsch, BreAnn. *Abraham Lincoln*. Minneapolis: Abdo Publishing, 2021.

NOTE TO EDUCATORS

Visit **www.focusreaders.com** to find lesson plans, activities, links, and other resources related to this title.

Index

B
Black Americans, 16, 18, 20, 27

C
Civil War, 6, 18, 23–24
Congress, 11–12

D
Douglas, Stephen, 12

E
Emancipation Proclamation, 20

F
Fifteenth Amendment, 27
Fourteenth Amendment, 26

G
Gettysburg, 5–7

I
Illinois, 10, 12

J
Juneteenth, 20

R
Republican Party, 12–13

S
Senate, 12
slavery, 6, 15–19, 20, 24–26

T
Thirteenth Amendment, 26

U
Union, 18, 20

Answer Key: 1. Answers will vary; **2.** Answers will vary; **3.** B; **4.** B; **5.** B; **6.** C